SEASHELLS

A PORTRAIT OF THE ANIMAL WORLD

Andrew Cleave

NEW LINE BOOKS

Fax: (888) 719-7723
e-mail: info@newlinebooks.com

Printed and bound in China

ISBN 978-1-59764-365-8

Visit us on the web!
www.newlinebooks.com

Author: Andrew Cleave

Publisher: Robert Tod
Book Designer: Mark Weinberg
Production Coordinator: Heather Weigel
Senior Editor: Edward Douglas
Project Editor: Cynthia Sternau
Assistant Editor: Linda Greer
DTP Associate: Michael Walther
Typesetting: Command-O, NYC

All photographs by James H. Carmichael, Jr.

INTRODUCTION

Dusavel's cone shell, Conus dusaveli, *is found in deep water off the Philippines where it preys on other mollusks, but is itself sometimes swallowed by fish. It moves over reefs on a large foot which partly envelops the shell.*

There can be few natural objects as beautiful and fascinating as the shells of mollusks. No human sculptor can match the intricacies of design and patterns found in shells, some of which are so small that a magnifying glass is needed to fully appreciate their beauty. No artist can reproduce the stunning range of colors, markings, and textures seen in shells, which can very in size from a fraction of an inch (a few millimeters) up to giants over two feet in length (61 centimeters). Shells occur in all the world's oceans, from the polar regions to the tropics, and few beaches are found without some shells at the water line. Land and tree snails must be included also, for they, too, show the same beauties of form and color, and still more shells can be found in fresh water, in all habitats from the tiniest streams to the largest lakes.

Humans have used shells in many ways for thousands of years. Many of the largest mollusks are still important sources of food for coastal communities, and some, like abalones and oysters, are now expensive delicacies for gourmets. Shells have been used as jewelry, with some rare and particularly beautiful species commanding high prices. For some ancient cultures shells must have had a religious or ritual significance, for they have often been discovered by archaeologists investigating ancient tombs. It was usually high-ranking individuals like kings or priests who were buried with the most impressive shells. Numerous other uses have been discovered for shells; tools and kitchen utensils can be fashioned from them, and some have been used as a form of currency. The ancient Roman emperors wore

togas which had been dyed with a rich purple pigment extracted from the murex shell, a common species in the Mediterranean.

Shell collecting, a very popular pastime now, is not new. It is possible that the ancient Romans made shell collections; explorations of the ruins of Pompeii, buried by volcanic ash from the eruption of Vesuvius in 79 A.D., have revealed accumulations of shells of a variety of species. In seventeenth-century Europe, well-to-do people with the requisite time and money started to form large collections of the species known at the time, mainly those originating in the Mediterranean and the Caribbean. Elaborate display cabinets were built to house and show off the collections, and rare species were sold at auctions, with large sums of money changing hands. As more and more of the world's oceans and islands were explored, the range of shells available to collectors increased and the prices charged for them fell, making them accessible to far more people than the few wealthy collectors of the early years.

Today's shell collectors have the opportunity to study species from all around the world, but because of their sheer numbers they have a great responsibility to consider the conservation of the shells and their habitats. It should never be forgotten that a shell is the home of a living creature. If the shell is picked up empty on a beach, then clearly the once-living mollusk has finished with it, but if the shell still houses the organism which created it, the collector should consider very carefully who needs the shell most: Is the need for one more shell in the collection greater than the value of the life of the living thing inside it?

The endive murex, **Chicoreus chicoreum,** from the southwest Pacific, has a stout shell with short, curved, and slightly branched spines giving it a slight resemblance to the vegetable.

An empty shell of the Florida horse conch, **Pleuroplac gigantea,** lies abandoned in the surf on a lonely beach. Prizes like this often await the sharp-eyed collector, but the shell should be checked for other inhabitants as it could now be home to a hermit crab.

SHELL STRUCTURE

The basic building material of a shell is calcium carbonate, or chalk. With the addition of smaller amounts of other materials to harden it, the shell can grow and protect the mollusk throughout its life. Enveloping the soft living tissues of the mollusk is a membrane called the mantle which secretes the calcium carbonate to form the shell itself. Calcium carbonate present in the mollusk's environment eventually finds its way into the bloodstream and is then deposited by the mantle onto a tissue called conchiolin, which hardens to form the shell itself. In the living mollusk there is an outer layer called the periostracum which has the appearance of a brittle, semi-transparent skin. This is added to from the leading

Following page: A colorful selection of senatorial scallops, **Mimaclamys sentoria.** *The scallop is a bivalve, with a laterally compressed body and a shell consisting of two valves, or moveable pieces, joined by an elastic ligament.*

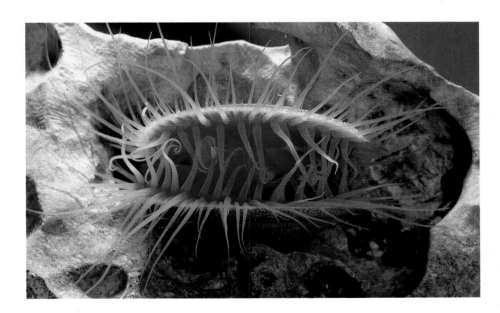

Loebbecke's murex, **Pterynotus loe-beckei,** *lives in 400- to 500-foot-deep water off the coasts of Japan, Taiwan, and the Philippines. The most striking features are the three waved wings which are rarely found without some damage. Most shells are a pale orange, but white and pink forms can also be found.*

This living file clam, **Lima scabra,** *uses its sinuous tentacles for both movement and defense. Potential predators are distracted by unpleasant secretions; the clam then makes a swift retreat to safer territory.*

Tulip shells, **Fasciolaria spp.,** *live offshore in sandy areas where they prey on other mollusks—usually bivalves, but sometimes their own kind. The shell shows many variations in texture, size, and colorings.*

Color and markings should never be used as the sole guide to identification, as is illustrated by the variation in these common and rosy phos shells, **Phos senticosus** *and* **roseatus.** *Other features such as shell shape, number of whorls, and details of the aperture should all be considered.*

edge by the mantle as the shell grows. Shells found washed ashore on a beach often lack this layer; the abrasive effect of sand and bleaching by the sun can lead to beached shells looking very washed-out and bearing little resemblance to the brightly colored living shells. The inner layer of the shell is often beautifully colored and very smooth; this is the result of the presence of a thin layer of nacre, or mother-of-pearl. This provides a comfortable environment for the mollusk to live in. The nacre will coat irritant objects which enter the shell, the best known example being the pearls formed inside oysters. If a tiny grain of sand enters the shell it will irritate the delicate mantle tissues, so nacre is

secreted to cover it. This grows and grows until eventually a large pearl is formed.

The immense variety of forms of shells is the result of millions of years of evolution. Although in our eyes some of the shells may seem to be unnecessarily adorned with spirals, projections, coils, or other structures, there is a very good reason for them. During the course of evolution, structures which serve no function will not survive. Structures which make a mollusk less successful in its environment will probably lead to its failure to breed or early capture by predators, so only those mollusks which possess all the features necessary for survival in a harsh and uncompromising world will live long enough to

An extremely rare deep-water **Sthenorytis turbinum,** *or turban wentletrap, from the Galapagos Islands. The shell of the wentletrap is constructed like a winding staircase, with a descending spiral of raised ribs.*

The unusual uncoiled shell of Miller's nutmeg, Trigonostoma milleri, is rare among the gastropod mollusks. This species lives in very deep water off the coasts of Mexico and Galapagos, where it seems to prefer muddy seabeds.

breed and pass on those features to the next generation. The murex shell, for example, has many long, pointed projections which are decorative to our eyes, and may appear to make the shell more cumbersome when moving along the seabed, but to a hungry fish they will represent a tough challenge. Trying to break open a shell with such armor is almost impossible, so the murex is usually left alone and a less well-armored species will be chosen as food.

Some shells clearly appear to be made of calcium carbonate, due to their chalky appearance, but many are richly colored and patterned. Some of the coloring is due to the pigments available in the mollusk's diet; in the warmer regions of the world, where food is abundant and varied, some of the most colorful mollusks can be found. Coloring in shells probably has little to do with warning or camouflage, the shell itself being protection enough in most cases. The brilliant colors of some shells are a surprise to some people who may only be familiar with the worn and faded specimens found on a beach. It is only the living mollusk which will show its true colors.

Classifying Shells

To the casual observer of shells, there are two main types: the gastropods, or those which live in a single shell, such as a whelk; and the bivalves, or those which live in a pair of hinged shells, such as a clam. There are in

The strongly ribbed shell of Mercado's nutmeg, *Scalptia mercadoi*, is a defense against attacks by crabs. This species inhabits deep water off the Philippines, and is itself a predator of other species of reef-dwelling animals.

The textile cone, *Conus textile*, is a mollusk which can inflict a dangerous and sometimes fatal sting on humans, so live specimens of this species should never be picked up. The "sting" is the radula, which it uses to paralyze its prey.

Kiener's delphinula, Angaria sphaerula, from reefs off the Philippines, has a more symmetrical shape, but it is still protected by the rigid spines seen in other species.

The tulip shell preys on other mollusks, including, sometimes, its own kind. Moving along on its muscular foot, it searches for a mollusk which it can feed on by drilling through the shell with its radula. Note the operculum, or horny trap door attached to the trailing end of the foot.

One of the rarer species of latiaxis shells is the Santa Cruz latiaxis, Babelomurex santacruzensis, found only off the island of Santa Cruz, Galapagos, where it is restricted to deep water. These are coral-feeding species which are only found where there is a plentiful supply of soft corals.

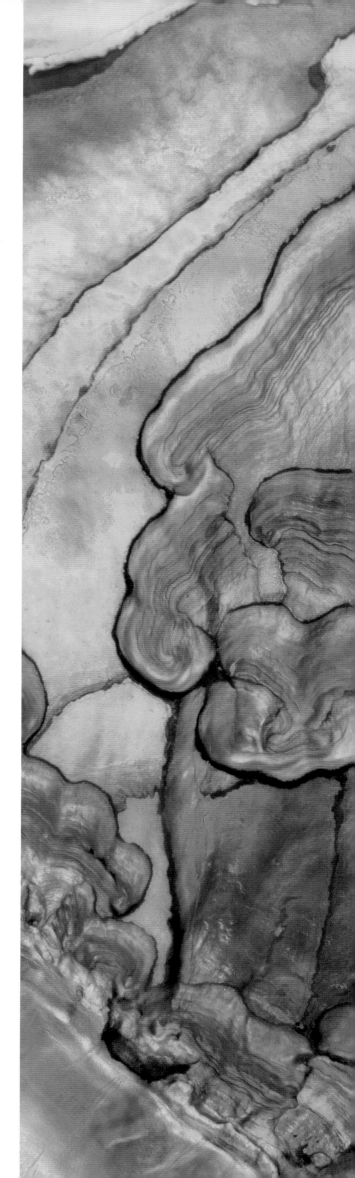

The hawkwing conch, Strombus ranius, from
the Caribbean region, is another variable species,
with several color forms shown here. The shell is
solid and armed with short, stout spines.

The shell of the abalone exhibits some of the
most beautiful colors in nature, but they are
rarely seen in the wild due to the shell's covering
of debris and other small living creatures.

The angular triton, Cymatium femorale, *widespread across the Caribbean region and the Bahamas, is usually found in shallow water among eelgrasses. As with the other tritons,the shell is covered with a thick periostracum in life, making it very difficult to locate.*

Deep water off the northwest coast of Australia is the main area where Bednall's volute, Volutoconus bednalli, *occurs. This species is not often seen, but can be recognized by the network of dark lines on its otherwise plain shell.*

fact several other classes of mollusks, but these are of little interest to the shell collector. The cephalopods are unlikely looking mollusks. These include the squids, cuttlefish, and octopus, which have a chalky internal "bone" to give them support. The nautilus is a cephalopod which looks like a cross between an octopus and a gastropod with its thin, coiled shell. This is provided with several gas-filled chambers for buoyancy. The nautilus is a present-day relative of the ammonite, a familiar fossil which was found in our oceans 300 million years ago. Three further classes of mollusks exist, but they are not as numerous as the main classes. The tusk shells, or scaphopods, live inside simple long, hollow shells which are usually white when encountered on the beach, but may be more colorful in life. They dwell in silty sand and are not often seen. The coat-of-mail shells, or chitons, are widespread along rocky shorelines in many parts of the world. Their shells consist of eight armored plates and they are often disguised by a thin growth of algae. They are of little interest to collectors as the colors rarely last after the death of the mollusk. Their resemblance to giant tropical cockroaches has led to their alternative South American name of *cucarachas del mar* or "sea cockroaches." The final group, the monoplacophorans, or gastroverms, are very simple mollusks with tiny shells covering only part of their worm-like bodies. They inhabit the deepest oceans and so are rarely seen.

The thin, pear-shaped shell of the fig-shell, **Ficus communis,** *is not often seen in life as the mollusk normally lives under sand, and the mantle partly covers the shell when the mollusk is active. It has a particularly large foot and head with well-developed tentacles.*

THE GASTROPODS

Gastropods are probably better known as snails. These are mollusks which have a single shell, usually growing in a spiral. Their name comes from the Latin words for stomach and foot, because they appear to be crawling along on fleshy stomachs. There may be as many as eighty thousand species of gastropods, most of which have shells. Some, like the slugs, have greatly reduced shells or, more commonly, no shells at all. The sea slugs, or nudibranchs, despite their lack of shells, can be very beautiful creatures with wonderful coloring and flowing body lines.

Most shelled gastropods can retract fully into their shells if danger threatens, emerging to feed or move when safe. At the leading end of the muscular foot is the head, which usually supports a pair of stalked eyes and the mouth. As the mollusk grows the mantle secretes more calcium carbonate, which is deposited near the leading edge. It grows in an ever-widening spiral, so the area of shell nearest the opening is the youngest and the area near the center or tip of the spiral is the oldest. This can often show signs of wear in older specimens, or it may even be colonized by simple algae.

Gastropods feed in several different ways. Some, like limpets and periwinkles, simply graze algae from the surfaces of rocks and plants. They have a rough tongue which is swept over the surface, scraping off tiny particles of food. The tongue, or radula, is usually coiled up inside the head, and as it wears away due to the constant abrasion on other surfaces, it uncoils slowly so the mollusk can continue feeding. Many gastropods are predators which attack other living things. These are often armed with a much more powerful radula which behaves more like a drill, and is capable of making holes in the shells of other mollusks, or the chalky skin, or test, of a sea urchin. It is often aided by a secretion, an acid which can help to dissolve the prey animal's shell. The drilling process may take several hours or even days, according to the toughness of the prey animal's shell. If the prey is a bivalve mollusk it will have no means of escape; it will have to remain in a fixed position, awaiting its fate. Some of the predatory gastropods, such as the cone shells, have a long proboscis which paralyses the prey

Tapestry turban shells, **Turbo petholatus,** *show a wide range of elaborate patterning on their shells, but an especially interesting feature is the hard, shiny operculum with its green "cat's eye" in the center.*

Victor Dan's miter shell, **Scabriola vicdani,** *is one of many similar species of predatory mollusks which have the miter-shaped shell vaguely resembling a bishop's hat. They all prey on other mollusks or worms, and have a powerful venom to immobilize them.*

The long groove in the shell of Hirase's slit shell, Perotrochus hirasei, is not a result of damage or predation; it is there to allow the living mollusk to get rid of waste matter. Slit shells live in deep water and feed on marine sponges.

so that they can feed on it at their leisure. Live cone shells should not be picked up, as some species can inflict a very painful, and sometimes fatal, wound on human skin.

Slit Shells

The simplest of all the gastropods are the slit shells, which have a groove in the shell used to aid the removal of wastes. In all other respects they look like normal gastropods. Some may reach a size of 10 to 12 inches (25 to 30 centimeters) but most are much smaller.

Abalones are most well known as seafood delicacies, and as a result of overfishing they are becoming increasingly scarce. They have a series of circular openings along the shell to help in the removal of waste matter. As the shell grows new openings appear, but older ones close over, so there are always the same number of openings in a given species. The inside of the shell has a striking pearly luster, but the outer surface is very dull by comparison. If this outer layer is removed, however, the same brilliant colors are revealed. As a result of the importance of this species to commercial fishermen, some marine biologists in California have attempted to farm abalones. This has proved to be successful enough to provide sufficient abalones to export to Japan. The abalone is a significant food species for the sea otter, so it is important that this mollusk is allowed to thrive.

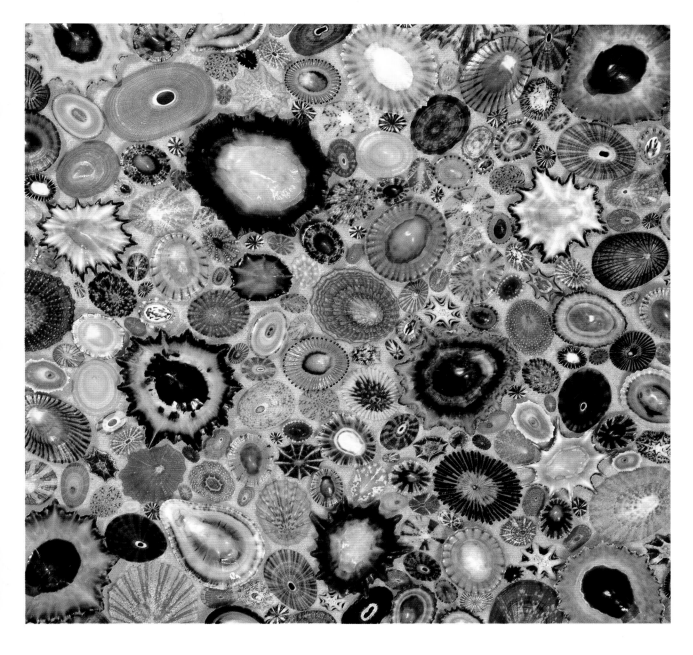

Limpets

Limpets will be very familiar to anyone who has wandered along a rocky shoreline at low tide. Their squat, conical shapes and tough, muscular foot enable them to hold on in the roughest of seas, so they are capable of survival in the sort of conditions where other mollusks would soon be swept away. Limpets always use the same resting place on the rock, nestling down in exactly the same position every time they return. Eventually their shells grow to fit the contours of the rocks, so they fit perfectly. On some soft rocks, such as shale and limestone, they can wear the rocks away slightly, leaving a small depression to give them an even more secure foothold.

Limpets graze on algae and have a rough tongue, or radula, to help them rasp tiny plants off the rocks. They have favored feeding areas, and sometimes drive other mollusk species away from their own feeding areas. Time-lapse photography, which condenses a day's activities in a few minutes' film time, reveals the limpet's battles when threatened by rivals. There is much jostling and shoving if an invader is detected, and the limpet, which appears to us to be almost stationery, does not rest until the intruder has been repelled. The simple conical shape is often adorned by bright colors, usually at their best on the inner surface. It is often necessary to study the inside of the shell to

A collection of abalone shells shows the variation that exists among the different species. One of the largest is the northern green abalone (top left), and one of the most colorful is the Australian species, Emma's abalone (bottom left), which has beautiful red markings.

Kiener's delphinula is a rather delicate species which is often found with damaged spines. Its colors can vary from green through red. It lives in deep water in the tropical Pacific and is sometimes encountered by fishermen hauling in nets over reefs.

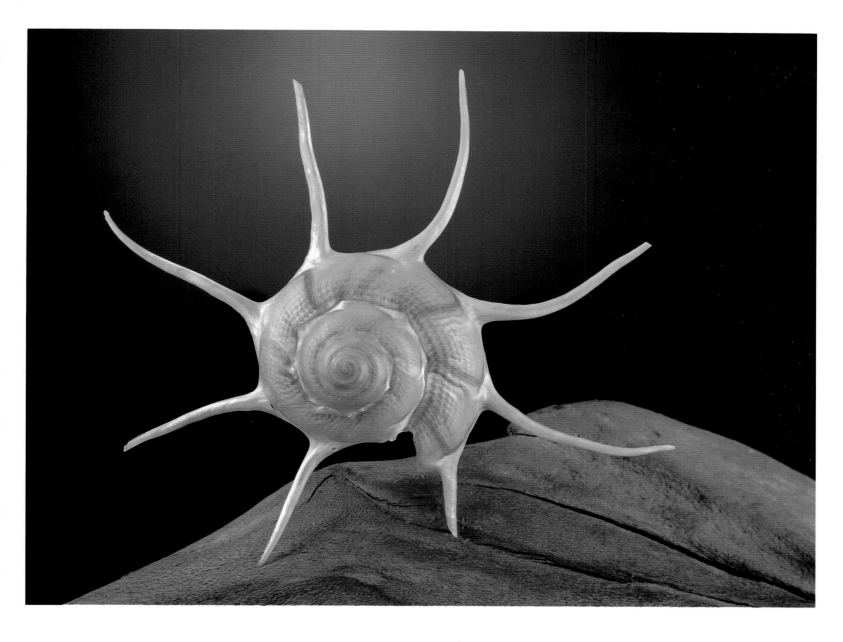

identify it correctly—the outer surface is often covered with minute algae in live limpets. Some limpets have an opening in the top of the shell; these are the keyhole limpets, which use the opening as a means of removing wastes.

Top and Turban Shells

Top shells bear a superficial resemblance to a child's spinning top, having a perfectly pointed conical shape. Some are quite large and are gathered for food, and some have shells thick enough to yield commercial quantities of mother-of-pearl. Living top shells have an operculum, or trap-door structure which can close over the mouth of the shell when the animal retreats inside. The operculum is attached to the foot and is slightly flexible. Most top shells are grazers, preferring rocky shores where they can feed on algae growing on rocks or seagrasses. A few species are carnivorous, preying mainly on soft-bodied creatures like anemones or sea slugs. Several species can be found on the seashore, but some live at great depths and are only seen when dredged up in trawls.

Turban shells also have a resemblance to tops, but their shape is more rounded and they are usually restricted to tropical reefs and deeper water than top shells. Some have elaborate projections on the ridges, giving them a star-like appearance. Divers or snorkelers may sometimes come across turban shells when exploring reefs, but they usually hide themselves in crevices during the brightest part of the day.

The Yoka star turban, **Gildfordia yoka,** *lives in very deep water where the seabed is silty. It is possible that the delicate spines help keep it on the surface of the fine silt, as well as protecting it from predators. As a further protection the star turban has a very thick operculum to close its shell.*

One of these ringed top shells, Calliostoma annulatum, *shows the operculum, or horny plate which acts as a trap door to protect the living mollusk inside its shell.*

The resemblance to a child's spinning top gave the top shells their common name. They all have a neat conical shape and sharply pointed tip, and most species have colorful markings. Top shells graze on microscopic algae and are nearly always found on rocky seashores and reefs. Shown is the striped top, Trochus virgatus.

The imperial delphinula, **Angaria delphinus**, *from the Philippines, has an extraordinary shape with an almost tubular shell protected by numerous thick, spiny projections which would make it a most unpleasant meal for a hungry fish. The opening of the aperture has a fine layer of mother-of-pearl. It feeds on algae on rocks in shallow water.*

The attractive sunburst star turban shell, **Astrea heliotropium***, is a species found in deep water off the coast of New Zealand; the first specimen was discovered by Captain Cook in the eighteenth century. In life the shell is covered with encrustations, and the star-like structure is not clearly visible.*

Pheasant Shells and Nerites

Pheasant shells are small, periwinkle-like species in colder waters, but in the tropics they grow to a larger size and have beautiful markings. Most pheasant shells live in sheltered bays and lagoons, feeding on microscopic algae and sea grasses.

Nerites are small, rounded shells, common in the tropics on rocky shores and among mangrove roots. The shells are mostly uniform in size; some have what appear to be teeth inside the opening. What they lack in size and shell shape they more than compensate for in the immense variety of colors and patterns seen even within a single species. The zig-zag nerite, a common mangrove species, has a most striking pattern of black and white lines on the shell, and no two seem to be alike. One of the smallest nerites is the Pacific emerald, which is rarely more than a quarter of an inch long (5 millimeters) and is easily overlooked among the seagrasses it feeds on; it is one of the few shells which shows a true green coloration.

*The Pacific emerald nerite, **Smaradgia rangiana**, is noteworthy for the beautiful shade of green, unusual among mollusks, on its tiny shell. It lives among eelgrasses, so this color affords it effective camouflage.*

*The bleeding tooth nerite, **Nerita peloronta**, is an easy species to identify because of the striking markings and two "teeth" inside the aperture. Like all nerites, there is great color variation within this single species.*

Periwinkles and Conchs

Periwinkles are a very important group of gastropods, although many are rather drab in appearance. They are mostly quite small and colored so that they blend in with the rocks and seaweeds on the intertidal zone of the seashore. They feed on algae and detritus and have developed many adaptations to living in a harsh environment. Many are tolerant of long periods of exposure to the air, and some can live in water of low salinity such as that in estuaries and harbors. They are prized in some parts of Europe as delicacies, with large numbers collected and then cooked for human consumption. A few, such as the flat periwinkle, have colored and banded shells, but most, in their living state, are easily over-looked.

The conch family is very well known, for some of the largest and most beautiful of the gastropods are conchs. They are all grazing mollusks, feeding on microscopic algae which coat sheltered sandy seabeds and sea grasses. Where not taken by collectors they live in colonies and can be seen plowing through the seabed on their large "feet."

The scorpion conch, **Lambis scorpius,** *widespread in the Indo-Pacific region, is a very colorful species with a rich combination of orange and purple markings inside the aperture. Most specimens have very long curved spines, which develop with age.*

The West Indian fighting conch, **Strombus pugilus,** *has a very strong shell with short, tough projections around the spire. Sometimes groups of up to three hundred of these shells can be seen plowing through the sand in shallow water. The shell is protected on the outside by a thick, semi-transparent skin.*

33

Conchs are unusual among gastropods in having a notch in the shell through which the right eye protrudes on a stalk. The left eye emerges on its stalk through the siphonal canal. The operculum is adapted for pushing through the sand, and in some of the small species the operculum and foot combined make an efficient means of locomotion, strong enough to allow the conch to jump clear of predators. Conch shells are highly prized by collectors, especially some of the larger species such as the queen conch from Florida, and the flesh of many is edible. For such large mollusks, they have a surprisingly short life span, with a three- to four-year life cycle typical for the queen conch. Large numbers of conch shells are dredged up by nets from tropical waters such as those surrounding the Philippines. Usually they are cleaned up and sold to collectors, but in some cases the flesh is consumed first. The spider conch resembles some of the murex shells, with long tough projections on the shell to protect it from predatory fish.

Granulated conch shells, Strombus granulata, *are usually found in lagoons and shallow water where there are plenty of seagrasses, but they also occur in deeper water; these unusually colorful specimens were dredged up off the west coast of Panama.*

Periwinkles are very common seashore and shallow-water mollusks which rarely reach a large size, but can be abundant in suitable habitats. They feed on algae and detritus on rocks, and many can live out of water for several hours at a time.

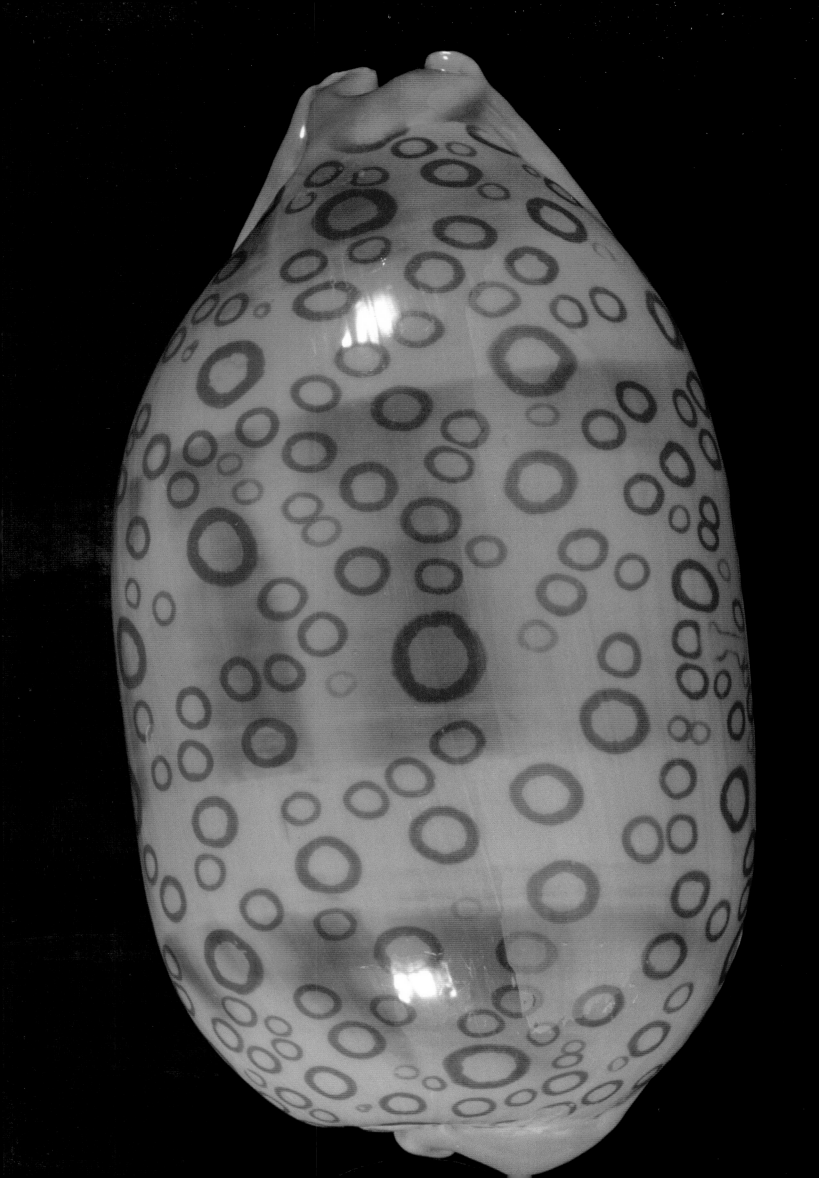

Cowries

The cowries are a very well-known family and have been familiar to people in coastal regions of the world for several thousand years. It is known that one species was used as a form of currency in China around four thousand years ago, and that they were used in India, Arabia, and Africa as well, with tons of shells being traded for vast sums of money. In addition to their significance as a form of currency, cowries also had a role as fertility symbols in places as far apart as Japan, China, and Africa. To some people the cowrie was seen as a protection against evil, and real cowries, clay models, and pictures of them were included in buildings and tombs; some of the ancient Egyptian burials included cowries. The tiger cowrie is probably the most familiar of all the species as its relatively large size, shiny surface, and boldly spotted shell make it an attractive object to even the most casual observer. It is found on reefs in the Indo-Pacific region and exported by the ton to Europe for sale in shell shops. Cowries are predators, feeding on soft-bodied rock-dwelling creatures like star ascidians. The foot almost envelops the shell as the animal moves, and the siphon sticks up in front of the shell like a tiny periscope. Female cowries lay their eggs in tiny capsules which they fix

to rocks in clusters. They then guard these capsules by covering them with their foot until they hatch. Tiny free-swimming larvae called veligers emerge, which swim to the upper layers of the ocean. They have two tiny, fin-like flaps to help them swim, but they are at the mercy of the ocean currents and so can be dispersed over a wide area. The veligers feed on plankton, and as they grow their shells develop. Eventually they become too heavy to keep swim-

The golden cowrie, Cypraea aurantia, is an elusive species of the Pacific reefs, where it remains hidden during the day in rock crevices, only emerging cautiously at night to feed. A live cowrie covers the rich orange color of its shell with its mantle, but when alarmed it withdraws inside and reveals its shell.

The white-spotted cowrie, Cypraea guttata, is a deep-water species found off Papua New Guinea and the Philippines. It has an unusual pattern of dark red lines blending in with the orange on the top of the shell. Note the tiny specimens of Marie's cowrie, from the central Pacific region, in the foreground.

The eyed cowrie, Cypraea argus, common throughout the Indo-Pacific, is easily recognized with its pattern of rings. No two shells are the same, and there is great variation in the size, number, and intensity of the rings.

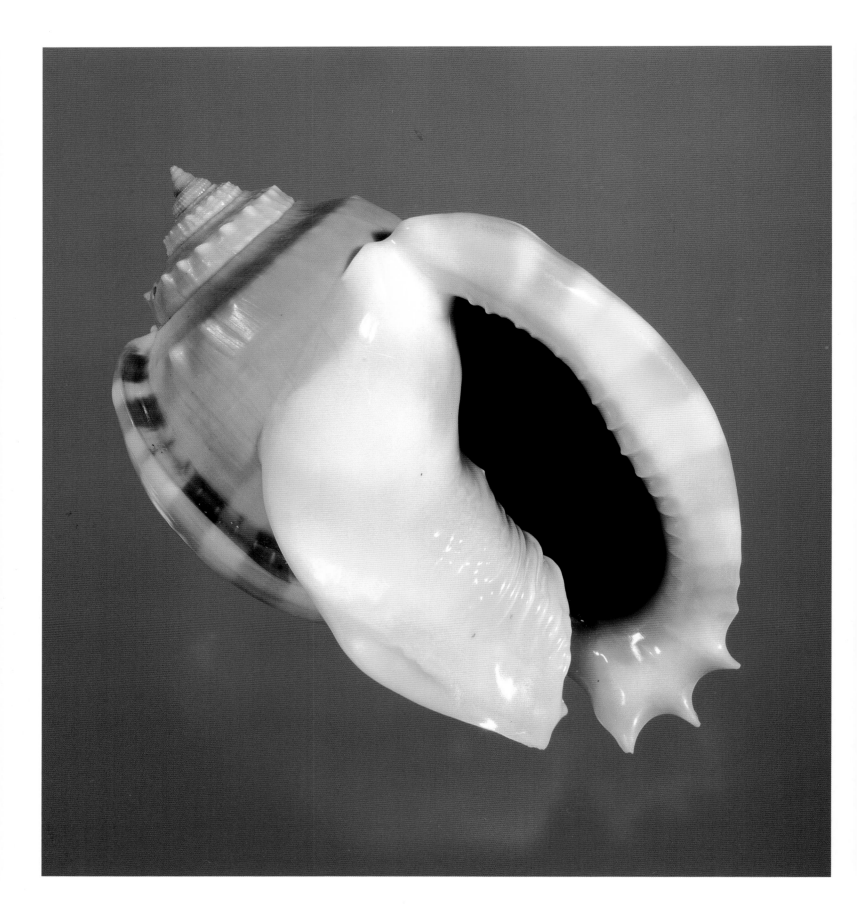

Like the helmet shells, the gray bonnet shell, Phalium glaucum, is a predator of sea urchins and sand dollars, and is found in warmer parts of the Indo-Pacific region. It is recognized by the spiny edge on the outer lip of the shell.

ming and sink toward the seabed. Many will settle down in completely unsuitable places and die, but enough will find reefs where there is sufficient food and survive to become full-grown adults.

Helmets

Helmet shells are large, thick shells which usually have a prominent, glossy lip. The living mollusk plows its way through sand and silt in search of partly buried sea urchins and sand dollars. These are enveloped by the large foot and then immobilized by a strong toxin, injected into their bodies through a hole drilled by the mollusk's radula. The internal organs of the prey are digested and then sucked out by the helmet through the hole drilled in the shell. Some helmets have such a thick shell, consisting of layers of different colors, that they can be used for carving cameos, a practice which came into prominence in eighteenth-century Europe. Cutting through the white outer layer reveals a brown layer beneath, making it possible to carve intricate works of art. One of the largest species of helmets is the queen helmet, found off many Caribbean islands. Like most of the other hel-

met shells, this mollusk remains hidden during the day and only becomes active at night, so despite weighing several pounds and having a very large shell, its secretive habits make it difficult to find. Similar species are the bonnet and false tun shells, most of which live in very deep water and feed in the same way as the helmet shells.

Tritons

Another well-known family of large shells is the tritons, or Ranellidae. These are

Helmet shells such as this horned helmet are predatory species which attack sea urchins and sand dollars by drilling into them with their radula and using digestive acids to break through their chalky skins. They are most active at night, feeding over sandy and muddy seabeds.

Following page: A strong triangular shape makes the king helmet shell, Cassis tuberosa, easy to recognize. The ridges on the shell are growth lines, formed by the animal burying itself in the sand and adding layers of new shell tissue.

Tritons are strong, thick-shelled mollusks which have a predatory way of life. They feed on other mollusks and marine invertebrates such as starfish, paralyzing them by injecting a powerful narcotic into their bodies. This ridged African triton is found off the coasts of South Africa.

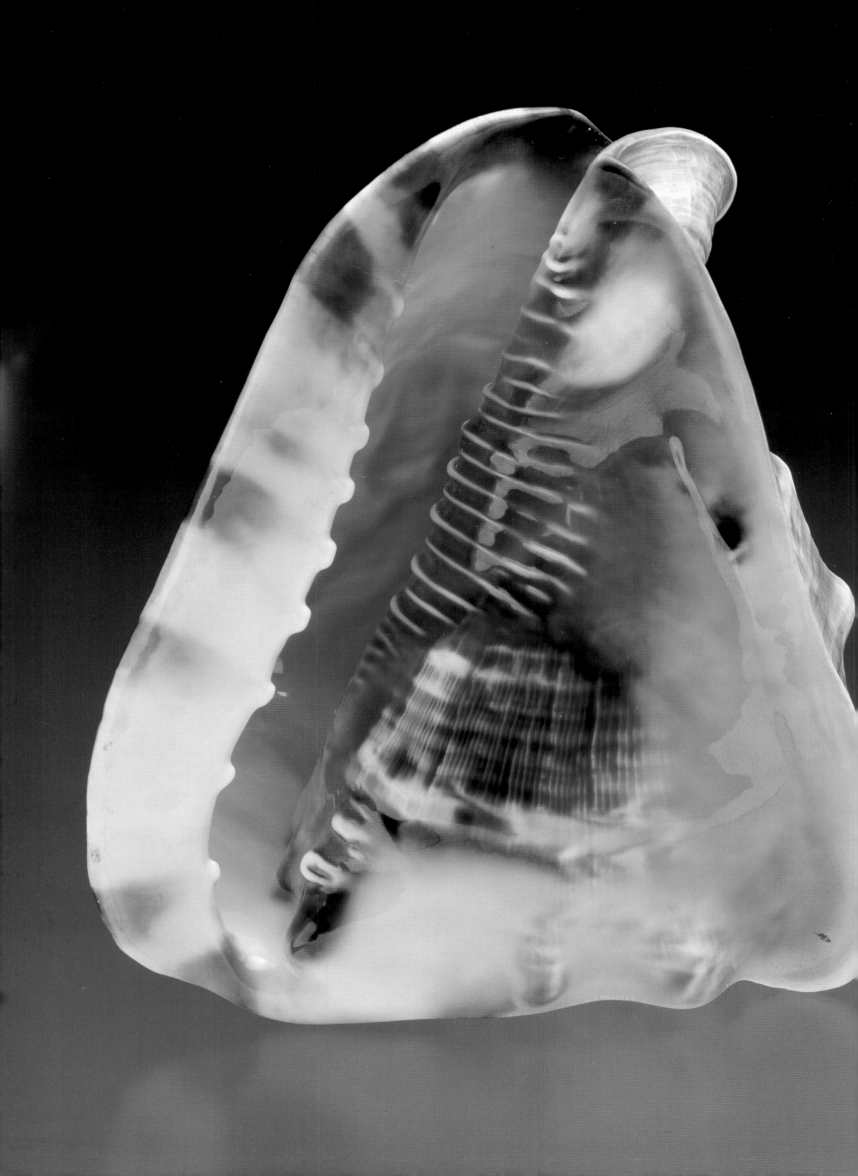

found worldwide, and some species are very large and attractive. They are all predators, taking a wide variety of other marine organisms, including other mollusks, urchins, worms, crabs, and fish. They are armed with a powerful radula to inject their venom and a strong muscular foot in order to be able to pursue their prey. A formerly common species is the Atlantic trumpet triton, so called because with the tip filed off the shell, it can be blown like a horn. Its habit of living in shallow water has made it very vulnerable to collectors, so it is threatened in some areas. Tritons, like many mollusks, produce large numbers of tiny free-swimming larvae, which in this family are very tolerant of changing conditions, so they can be carried over great distances by ocean currents.

Wentletraps

Wentletraps have a superficial resemblance to a spiral staircase, and it is this which gives them their common name, derived from the Dutch *wenteltrappe* for "winding stairs." They have a very wide distribution, occurring in all oceans, and there may be over seven hundred species. The largest is the three-inch-long precious wentletrap from the Philippines, Taiwan, and Sri Lanka. Its rarity in the past led to extraordinarily accurate fakes being fashioned from rice paste and sold to collectors for large sums of money. Wentletraps are predators which attack soft-bodied creatures like sea anemones, sucking out their body fluids. Living in deep water, they are rarely seen, but are thought in some places to exist in very large populations; sometimes beaches can be littered with hundreds of their empty shells after a storm.

The black-spotted triton, **Cymatium lotorium,** *has a strong, thick shell, an adaptation to the exposed conditions in which it lives. It normally occurs on rocky reefs where it is likely to be tumbled around by waves.*

Left: Although it is relatively small and uniformly colored, the precious wendletrap, **Epitonium scalare,** *has a beautifully sculptured shell with conspicuous ribs running along the loose coils.*

Murexes

The murexes are noted for their highly sculptured shells with elaborate spines and scales. These can be colorful, although most are rather plain, but they nearly always lack markings and patterns. They can be found in most of the world's oceans, with some fine specimens occurring in the Mediterranean and off the coast of Australia. Most are predators and can be abundant on oyster and mussel beds, where they may have a serious effect on their populations. Some act as scavengers and search the seabed for animal remains.

Murexes were prized in ancient times for the dye that they yielded. The imperial purple, which only royalty were entitled to wear, was obtained from the murexes common in the Mediterranean. Many of the murexes

Flinder's vase shell, **Altivasum flindersi**, *is a magnificent species from deep water off the southern coast of Australia. It is rarely encountered, but occasionally turns up in baited crab pots or trawl nets. It preys on worms and mollusks, and can withdraw completely into its shell, which it closes with an operculum.*

produce a substance called punicin which helps harden the outer case of their egg capsules and is also thought to render the mollusk unpalatable to other predators. If the punicin is exposed to the air it turns from a milky white, through yellow-green, to a deep purple. This change is permanent and an excellent dye is produced. Immense numbers of murexes were needed to produce a few pounds of dye, a process which took several days of crushing, boiling, and refining. To this day, mountainous piles of murex shell debris can be found on parts of the Mediterranean coastline, especially at what is now Lebanon. Curiously, at the same time that the early Minoans on Crete were developing the technology to produce the royal purple dye, the pre-Columbian Indians on the Mexican coast were also extracting dyes from murexes. Rock shells and drupes are closely related to the murexes, but they are smaller, more compact, and much harder to see due to their covering of algae; some of these also yield dyes. The latiaxis shells bear a superficial resemblance to murexes, but they are much more delicate and usually rarer, being confined to deep water and, in some cases, only single localities.

Variations in depth, wave action, and currents lead to variations in the appearance of the lace murex, **Chicoreus florifer.** *Calm conditions allow it to develop many large projections on the shell, but in more exposed areas it has fewer projections and a thicker, stronger shell. This species is found in the Caribbean region and the Bahamas.*

Like all the murex shells, the Venus comb murex, **Murex pecten**, is known more for the fantastic shape of the shell than the color or luster of its surface. It is unique among shells in having a mass of needle-like spines giving it the appearance of a comb or a fish bone. It is a widespread Indo-Pacific species, but finding a perfect specimen with unbroken spines is very unusual.

Saul's murex, **Chicoreus saulii**, is a very colorful species of the Philippines and surrounding areas. It lives on reefs in shallow water, but is not very common. Large specimens tend to be less colorful.

The dark spines on this endive murex contrast with the white shell, although in living specimens there are many encrustations on the shell which disguise the true colors.

Whelks

Over eight hundred species of whelks can be found around the world, with some of the largest species being found in the cold waters of the Arctic. These are usually rather dull in coloration and patterning, but with large, interestingly shaped shells. The tropical species are normally smaller but more colorful. Whelks are prized as a delicacy in many northern areas, and large quantities are dredged up and sold as food. Most whelks are scavengers and can be caught in baited pots, but a few are predators, attacking bivalves, crabs, and worms. The egg masses of some whelks are familiar objects on the shoreline after storms, consisting of several capsules joined together to form an orange mass of individual capsules. The young develop inside the capsule, with food provided in the form of extra, infertile eggs. Unlike many other mollusks, the tiny whelks which emerge from the capsules are miniature versions of the adults, with tiny shells. They are able to move away on a tiny foot and start feeding immediately, having bypassed the free-swimming larva stage of many other mollusks. Most whelk shells have a large opening without elaborate lips, and a strong siphonal canal.

Olive Shells

Olive shells bear a superficial resemblance to the shape of an olive. They are predators which attack worms and snails, but will also scavenge on dead animals. Their prey is usually enveloped by the foot and dragged under the sand. There is little variation in the shell shape between the various species, but a tremendous variety in the markings. Most olive shells are found in shallow, tropical waters, often over sandy seabeds.

Neptune shells are large, predatory species found in colder waters; this many-ribbed neptune, Neptunea polycostata, *lives in deep water off the northern coast of Japan, where it sometimes enters baited crab and lobster pots.*

Miter and Harp Shells

A bishop's miter was the inspiration for the name of the miter shells, all of which have a similar shape. They are all predators and can produce a powerful toxin with which to attack their prey; some can also secrete a purple dye. They are not restricted to a single habitat; as long as there is prey available they can be found on sand, over reefs, and on rocky shores, although most occur only in warmer regions of the Indo-Pacific.

A harp shell can be recognized very easily by the raised ribs along the shell which look similar to the strings of a harp. Harp shells are active predators of crabs and shrimps, which they search for over sandy seabeds. They may themselves be attacked by crabs, however, so the ribbed shell will be a defense here. An observation of a feeding harp shell offers an explanation of how it may defend itself: While being pursued by a box crab, a harp shell sheds a small piece of its foot which the crab then captures and starts to eat. While it is occupied doing this, the harp shell is able to overcome the crab by smothering it in a layer of mucus which soon becomes clogged with sand. The crab is then sucked dry by the harp shell!

There may be over five hundred species of miter shells worldwide, so considerable variation can be expected. The queen miters, Vexillum citrinum filiareginae (top), are among the most beautiful, and are occasionally found off the Philippines.

All species of harp shells show the raised ribs on the shell, but their size and colorings vary considerably between species. They are predators, feeding by gliding over sand and mud in search of smaller creatures which they envelop.

The imperial harp shell, **Harpa costata**, like other members of this family, gained its name from the string-like raised ribs running along the shell. This species is one of the most magnificent, and is given special protection in its main site some distance off the coast of Mauritius.

The needle-like auger shells live in sandy areas where they can burrow easily in search of worms, which they paralyze with a venom before ingesting them whole. They are mostly shorter than two inches (5 centimeters), but a few species can be more than twice this length.

The music volute is restricted to shallow seas with sandy seabeds in the southern Caribbean region. Its common name derives from the appearance of a musical score formed by the variable brownish lines and patches on the creamy white shell.

Volutes

Volutes are secretive mollusks which live buried in sand for much of the time and only emerge at night to feed. They have elegant, streamlined shells, often very glossy and well-patterned, and can reach a length of up to 9 or 10 inches (23 to 25 centimeters). They are among the few species which do not produce free-swimming larvae, so as a result, individual species are not widely distributed. Tiny, fully formed volutes emerge from egg capsules, and one species actually appears to produce live young; in fact, the egg capsules are retained inside a special pouch in the foot where they are protected until they can fend for themselves. The foot is very large and often beautifully patterned. It is used to surround the prey—normally a small bivalve mollusk—which is poisoned and digested by venomous saliva. Volutes are found in the Atlantic and Indo-Pacific regions; some species are very rare.

Not all gastropods have tightly coiled shells of a conventional shape. The tiny Miller's nutmeg shells have a more worm-like appearance with open coils, although some of the other nutmegs look slightly more like other gastropods. These deep-water species are carnivores, but much of their lives is a mystery due to their difficult habitat.

Ponsonby's volute, **Festilyria ponsonbyi,** *is one of the larger shells of the African coast. An uncommon species, it inhabits shallow water, usually where the seabed consists of coral sand or silt through which it plows in search of food. Like all the volutes, it has a very thick shell.*

Cone and Sundial Shells

The cone shells are well known for their habit of stunning their prey with a powerful venom. They have a good sense of smell to enable them to locate their prey, and a long proboscis with a sharp tooth at the end which penetrates the prey animal's body so that the venom can be injected. Small prey animals are swallowed whole and digested inside the cone's body. When digestion is complete, any tough remains such as shells or bones are ejected. Worms are a favorite prey, but fish and other mollusks are taken by some species. In some particularly rich habitats many species of cone shells will be found, each one specializing in a different prey animal. The proboscis, bearing the venomous tooth, shoots out of the narrower end of the shell, but in some species the proboscis is long enough to snake back as far as the blunt end. It is advisable not to pick up live cone shells, as several human deaths have been recorded, as well as numerous very painful stings. Medical research into this venom has shown that there may be some useful drugs, such as muscle relaxants or stimulants, to be obtained from them. Cone shells can be found in abundance in some tropical waters, but few species have a very wide range. Although a large number of cones may appear to be present in one area, they may be of several different species, some of which could be quite rare.

Sundial shells are recognized by their flattened shape and central umbilicus which runs through the middle of the spiral. They are found in the Indo-Pacific and Caribbean regions and most often feed on soft-bodied prey like sea anemones.

Sundial shells are very flattened and many have a central umbilicus, or hollow, around which the shell is coiled. They are found mainly in the Pacific and Caribbean regions where there are soft corals and anemones to feed on.

There is an immense variety of color forms and patterns even within a single species of cone shell. The magus cone, Conus magus (top), is very variable, and is found over huge areas of the Indo-Pacific region. It produces a powerful toxin for paralyzing its fish prey. The circumcision cone, Conus circumcisus, from Papua New Guinea and the Philippines, lives in rocky areas, and can reach a length of four inches (10 centimeters).

BIVALVES

There are around twenty thousand species of bivalves, or mollusks living in shells which are in two parts joined by a hinge. These are the clams, oysters, cockles, and mussels, many of them familiar as edible species. All of them are aquatic with most living in the sea, although many dwell in fresh water, in lakes and rivers. They range in size from minute pea cockles to the giant clam, and their shells can be plain or bear the most elaborate markings.

The two-part shell is joined by a tough but flexible hinge, and held closed by sets of muscles. Bivalves have a muscular foot which can emerge from the shell, but in most species it can be fully retracted and the shell can be tightly closed. If bivalves want to feed, breathe, or move, they must open the shell. Some have tubes, or siphons, which extend out of the shell and draw in currents of water bearing food and oxygen. One tube will act as an inhalation siphon and the other will be an exhalation siphon.

Bivalves often occur in immense numbers and are probably far more numerous than the

Many cockles are known as food species, with huge quantities harvested from sand flats in suitable areas. The shells are discarded, but many species show interesting variations in shell shape and patterning.

gastropods. In suitable habitats the seabed can be almost completely covered with tiny clams or tellins, and after storms some beaches can be piled high with their empty shells. Commercial fishing for cockles, clams, oysters, and scallops has been carried out for centuries and many species are very important for food. The production of pearls by

The fifty or so jewel-like eyes of the calico scallop, Argopecten gibbus, *show clearly around the inner edge of the open shell. Sensitive tentacles guarding the opening warn the scallop of possible intruders while its shell is open in the feeding position.*

The lion's paw scallop, Nodipecten nodosus, *has a knobbly, ridged shell, giving it its common name. It ranges widely in the Atlantic from Florida south to Brazil, and many color forms are found.*

Large numbers of strong overlapping scales give the shell of the fluted giant clam, Tridacna squamosa, *its frilled and rather delicate appeaance. These clams do not attain the great size of the giant clam, but live in similar habitats, fixed on coral reefs.*

oysters has led to them being cultivated on a vast scale in some areas, and huge sums of money are paid for some of the finest pearls.

Scallops have a classic shell shape which has been used in art and architecture for centuries. The ancient Greeks and Romans were especially attracted to the shape of the scallop shell and it features in many items of jewelry and works of art. It is also an important symbol in the Christian religion, representing St. James, the fisherman. Live scallops, with the two valves held apart, show two rows of eyes inside the shell. They are only simple structures, unable to form clear images like our eyes, but they can detect light and dark, they are sensitive to movement such as the sudden shadow caused by an approaching predator, and they can probably distinguish patches of light sand from darker rocks or seaweeds. Scallops normally rest on the seabed, but they can swim through the water by rapidly opening and closing the shell, moving in a series of little jumps. There are many species of scallops in all the world's

Few mollusks can exhibit such a range of colors and patterns as the bald scallop, Flexopecten glaber, *from the Mediterranean. Undamaged specimens often support a strange netting on the shell which resembles mountain scenery on a Japanese painting.*

Leafy, or Australian carditas, Cardita crassicosta, *are found off northern Australia and the Philippines, usually in shallow water over sand and gravel. Apart from the variety of bright colors, the shells also have fluted scales along the prominent ribs.*

oceans, and even within a single species there can be a great variety of colors and patterns.

Thorny oysters are rather inaccurately named, for they are not oysters at all, but more closely related to the scallops. Their shells bear numerous long spines and they are sometimes brightly colored. Some species are very difficult to see alive, as they are perfectly camouflaged on the seabed when the spines are coated with algae and debris. A few are highly prized as edible species.

Cardita clams are closely related to the cockles, which have fairly plain, tough shells. Like the cockles, they live almost completely buried in sand or mud, and like all the bivalves they are filter feeders. The heart cockle has an attractive heart-shaped shell when viewed from the side. Its delicate shell is semi-transparent and light can enter when it is in its normal position in shallow water on a reef. Tiny algae living inside the shell produce the food for the cockle in return for receiving protection inside its shell. Many cockles have thick shells, however, and find their food by filtering sea water. They are often found in river mouths and in shallow sandy areas where there are currents to keep them supplied with a constant supply of suspended material.

Tellins and donax clams are normally small, but they are nearly always very brightly colored. Their smooth, glossy shells enable them to slide easily through sand and mud to evade predators or find the best feeding positions. Unusually for bivalves, they tend to lie

Tellins are small burrowing bivalves which occur in sometimes phenomenal numbers in shallow sandy areas. Many of them lie in a horizontal position in the sand, and they have long siphons which they can push out to the surface to draw in water and food. The largest species shown in this selection is the foliated tellin, **Phylloda foliacea** *(top).*

on their sides in the sand, extending a long siphon up to the surface to find food. This sweeps around in a worm-like fashion sucking up food particles, while the shorter exhalation siphon removes the filtered waste water. The empty shells, showing a wonderful range of colors, can be found by the ton on some beaches, and northern waters are particularly rich in these species.

The strong ribs on the cloak scallop, **Gloripallium pallium**, *from the Pacific, have numerous tiny transverse ribs running across them, giving the shell a very rough texture.*

Cockle shells have symmetrical valves and fairly plain, smoothly ribbed shells. This giant African cockle, **Plagiocardium pseudolima**, *lives partly buried in sand in shallow water off much of the coast of East Africa. Most shells are pink, but paler specimens turn up occasionally.*

Following page: The Atlantic, or American thorny oyster, **Spondylus americanus**, *has many large projections on its shell which, when covered with other marine life, serve to camouflage and protect the living mollusk. It is more closely related to the scallop than the oyster.*

The fluted giant clam is a very large mollusk with a thick-ridged shell, although when it is in its usual position—fixed by tough byssus threads to corals—the shell is concealed. The mantle and other living tissues inside the shell have a green coloration due to the millions of microscopic algae living on them.

Vermilion scallops, Mimachlamys miniacea, inhabit sandy areas off the southern Philippines, with most showing some vermilion colorings. The shell is fairly smooth with close-set ribs.

Clams normally live buried in sand or mud, with only a small siphon emerging at the surface. They are filter feeders and can be present in vast numbers in suitable habitats. Their shells are normally smooth to aid burrowing, but they usually show interesting markings.

An array of circular scallops from the east Pacific further illustrate the variation found in these shells. Living specimens often support numerous other mollusks, crustaceans, worms, and seaweeds; some may even have encrustations of barnacles on their shells.

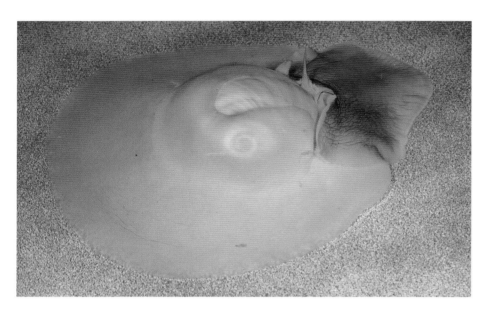

The moon snail is almost completely hidden by its mantle, the vital living membrane which secretes the chemical which makes up the shell.

The Nautilus Family

The nautilus is related to the cephalopods, which includes the more familiar squid and octopus. This is the only member of this family to have an external shell; it is rather like a living fossil, having survived more or less unchanged for 500 million years. There are five species found in the Pacific Ocean today. The living animal only occupies the front part of the shell, the remainder of it consisting of a series of connected chambers which are filled with a gas and a fluid. By altering the volume of the fluid in these chambers, the boyancy of the shell can be adjusted and the nautilus can rise and sink through the water with ease. It preys on small marine organisms such as crabs and shrimps, and will also scavenge for dead fish. It normally remains in quite deep water, but is fished for by some South Pacific islanders who consider the flesh a delicacy and use the shells for ornaments.

Slugs and Land Snails

Mollusks evolved in the sea and then colonized the land around 350 million years ago. Some have a lung-like chamber for breathing, while others have moist body surfaces for absorbing oxygen. Apart from the polar regions, land and tree snails can be found in all continents and in most habitats. The richest areas for them are the tropical forests, where the largest and most colorful species can be found. Slugs are mollusks which have

A section through the shell of a nautilus shows the series of chambers, filled with gas in life, and connected to the body of the mollusk through a tube, which controls its buoyancy. The nautilus is able to hover at any depth, or gracefully rise and sink through the water in search of food. Inhabiting deep areas of the Indo-Pacific, these usually remain about 600 feet (183 meters) below the surface.

A colorful selection of land and tree snails from around the world shows that not all of the attractive shells are confined to the oceans. Many of these terrestrial snails adopt bright coloration in order to blend in with flowers and leaves, and they often lack the encrustations covering many marine shells.

adapted to a way of life without a shell. They are often burrowers, or live in habitats where there is insufficient calcium to form a shell. Land and tree snails feed on a variety of plant material, ranging from microscopic algae, simple mosses, and liverworts, to flowering plants. Some scavenge on dead plant material or feed on fungi. There are a number of colorful and attractive species, some of which are prized by collectors. The green tree snail of Manus Island, off Papua New Guinea, is a delightful snail which has unfortunately suffered both from habitat loss and overcollecting. It is now a protected species, but little is being done to safeguard it. Several other land snails, such as the painted polymita of Cuba and the candy-stripe snail of Hispaniola, are in a similar position, and measures should be taken to protect them.

A Plea to Shell Collectors

Shells are such pleasing objects that they are, naturally, desirable for collections. Few people can resist the temptation to pick up empty shells from a beach and most will marvel at the beauty of what they see. There is lit-

tle harm in collecting abandoned empty shells from a beach, unless, of course, they are occupied by hermit crabs, but the wholesale collecting of living mollusks is a different matter. Many species are abundant and can tolerate some collecting pressure, but some are becoming very scarce and need time to recover. Collecting on its own is not the main reason for the decline of some mollusk species; our oceans are under threat from many other problems. Pollution and overfishing are very serious causes of damage to the environment; these are issues which must be tackled if mollusks, along with all other marine organisms from the great whales to the tiniest plankton, are to survive. Not only must shell collectors be aware of the problems of overcollecting, and take only what they really need, leaving rare species to recover, but they should also be on the lookout for damage to the environment. If future generations of shell collectors are to be given the chance to study these fascinating natural objects, the present generation should be prepared to fight to safeguard the habitats on which these creatures depend for their survival.

The tropid snails are all terrestrial species, usually found hiding under stones or in dense vegetation from which they emerge at night, or in damp conditions to feed on algae and simple plants. Cuvier's tropid snail, **Tropidophora cuvieriana**, *comes from the north of Madagascar.*

The colorful Cuban tree snail, or painted polymita, **Polymita picta**, *is restricted to low, shrubby vegetation in the east of Cuba, where it is a declining species due to habitat loss and over-collecting. At one time huge numbers were collected and turned into jewelry.*

INDEX

Page numbers in **bold-face** type indicate photo captions.

abalones, 16, 22, **26**
American (Atlantic) thorny oyster (*Spondylus americanus*), **63**
ammonites (fossil mollusk), 19
angular triton (*Cymatium femorale*), **18**
Atlantic (American) thorny oyster (*Spondylus americanus*), **63**
Atlantic trumpet triton, 43
auger shells, 52
Australian (leafy) carditas (*Cardita crassicosta*), **60**

bald scallop (*Flexopecten glaber*), **60**
Bednall's volute (*Volutoconus bednalli*), **18**
bivalves, 12, 59–63
  clams, **7, 60**, 66, 67
  cockles, 59, 63
  nautiluses, 19, 68, **68**
  oysters, 11
  scallops, **7**, 59, **60**, 63, 66, 67
  slugs and land snails, 21, 68–70, **69**, 70
black-spotted triton (*Cymatium lotorium*), **43**
bleeding tooth nerite (*Nerita peloronta*), **31**

calico scallop (*Argopecten gibbus*), 59
candy-stripe snail, 70
cardita clams, 63
  leafy (Australian) carditas (*Cardita crassicosta*), **60**
cephalopods, 19, 68
circular scallops, 67
circumcision cone (*Conus circumcisus*), **56**
clams, 59, 67
  cardita clams, **60**, 63
  file clam (*Lima scabra*), **7**
  fluted giant clam (*Tridacna squamosa*), **60**, 66
  classification of shells, 12–19
cloak scallop (*Gloripallium pallium*), **63**
coat-of-mail shells (chitons), 19
cockles, 59, 63
  giant African cockle (*Plagiocardium pseudolina*), **63**
collecting shells, 5, 70
coloring of shells, 12
conchiolin, 7
conchs, 33–34
  elongate (finger spinder conch; *Lambis digitata*), **23**
  Florida horse conch (*Pleuroplac gigantea*), 5
  graduated conch (*Strombus granulata*), 34
  hawkwing conch (*Strombus ranius*), **16**
  scorpion conch (*Lambis scorpius*), **33**
  West Indian fighting conch (*Strombus pugilus*), **33**
cone shells, 56, **56**
  Dusavel's cone (*Conus dusaveli*), **3**
  textile cone (*Conus textile*), **13**
Cook, James, 29
cowries, 37–39
  eyed cowrie (*Cypraea argus*), **37**
  white-spotted cowrie (*Cypraea guttata*), **37**
Cuban tree snail (painted polymita; *Polymita picta*), 70
Cuvier's tropid snail (*Tropidophora cuvieriana*), 70

donax clams, 63
Dusavel's cone (*Conus dusaveli*), **3**

elongate (finger spinder conch; *Lambis digitata*), **23**
Emma's abalone, **26**
endive murex (*Chicoreus chicoreum*), **5**, 46
evolution
  of mollusks, 68
  of shells, 11–12
eyed cowrie (*Cypraea argus*), **37**

feeding, by gastropods, 21–22
fig-shell (*Ficus communis*), 19
file clam (*Lima scabra*), **7**
finger spinder conch (elongate; *Lambis digitata*), **23**
Flinder's vase shell (*Altivasum fildersi*), **44**
Florida horse conch (*Pleuroplac gigantea*), 5
fluted giant clam (*Tridacna squamosa*), **60**, 66
foliated tellin, **63**
food
  abalones as, 22
  bivalves as, 59
  cockles as, 59
  conchs as, 34
  mollusks as, 3
  nautiluses as, 68
  periwinkles as, 33
  whelks as, 49

gastropods (snails), 12, 21–22
  cone and sundial shells, **3**, 13, 56, **56**
  cowries, 37–39, **37**
  helmets, 39, **39**
  limpets, 23–27, **23**
  miter and harp shells, **21**, 51, **51**
  murexes, **5**, 7, 12, 44–45, **45**, 46
  nutmeg shells, **12**, 13, 55
  olive shells, 49
  periwinkles and conchs, **5**, 16, 23, 33–34, **33**, 34
  pheasant shells and nerites, 31, **31**
  slit shells, 22, **22**
  top and turban shells, **21**, 27, 27–29
  tritons, 18, 39–43, **39**, **43**
  volutes, 18, **54**, 55, **55**
  wentletraps, 43, **43**
  whelks, 49
giant African cockle (*Plagiocardium pseudolina*), **63**
giant clams, **60**, 66
graduated conch (*Strombus granulata*), 34
gray bonnet shell (*Phalium glaucum*), **38**
green tree snail, 70

harp shells, 51, **51**
  imperial harp shell (*Harpa costata*), 52
hawkwing conch (*Strombus ranius*), **16**
heart cockles, 63
helmets, 39, **39**
Hirase's slit shell (*Perotrochus hirasei*), **22**
horned helmet, 39

Imperial delphinula (*Angaria delphinus*), **29**
imperial harp shell (*Harpa costata*), 52

Kiener's delphinula (*Angaria sphaerula*), **15**, 26
king helmet (*Cassis tuberosa*), **39**

lace murex (*Chicoreus florifer*), **45**
land snails, 68–70, **69**
  Cuvier's tropid snail (*Tropidophora cuvieriana*), 70
latiaxis shells, **15**
leafy (Australian) carditas (*Cardita crassicosta*), **60**
limpets, 23–27, **23**
lion's paw scallop (*Nodipecten nodosus*), 59
Loebecke's murex (*Pterynotus loebeckei*), **7**

magnus cone (*Conus magus*), **56**
many-ribbed neptune (*Neptunea polycostata*), 49
Marie's cowrie, 37
Mercado's nutmeg (*Scalptia mercadoi*), **13**
Miller's nutmeg (*Trigonostoma milleri*), **12**, 55
miter shells, 51, **51**
  Victor Dan's miter (*Scabriola vicdani*), **21**
mollusks
  bivalves, 59–70
  classifications of, 12–19
  collecting, 70
  shell structure of, 7–12
  used for food, 3
  see also gastropods
monoplacophorans (gastroverms), 19
moon snail, 68
mother-of-pearl (nacre), 11
murexes, 44–45
  endive murex (*Chicoreus chicoreum*), **5**, 46
  evolution of, 12
  lace murex (*Chicoreus florifer*), **45**
  Loebecke's murex (*Pterynotus loebeckei*), **7**
  Saul's murex (*Chicoreus saulii*), 46
  used as dye, 5
  Venus comb murex (*Murex pecten*), 46
music volute, **54**
mussels, 59

nacre (mother-of-pearl), 11
nautiluses, 19, 68, **68**
neptune shells, 49
nerites, 31
  bleeding tooth nerite (*Nerita peloronta*), **31**
  Pacific emerald nerite (*Smaragdia rangiana*), 31
nutmeg shells
  Mercado's nutmeg (*Scalptia mercadoi*), **13**
  Miller's nutmeg (*Trigonostoma milleri*), **12**, 55

olive shells, 49
oysters, 59–60
  pearls in, 11

Pacific emerald nerite (*Smaragdia rangiana*), 31
painted polymita (tree snail), 70
  Cuban tree snail (*Polymita picta*), 70
pearls, 11, 59–60

periostracum, 7–11
periwinkles, 33, **34**
pheasant shells, 31
phos shell (*Phos senticosus*), 10
Pompeii (ancient Rome), 5
Ponsonby's volute (*Festilyria ponsonbyi*), 55
precious wentletrap (*Epitonium scalare*), 43, **43**
punicin, 45

queen conch, 34
queen helmet, 39
queen miter (*Vexillum citrinum filiareginae*), 51

ridged African triton, 39
ringed top shell (*Calliostoma annulatum*), **28**
Rome, ancient, 3–5

Santa Cruz latiaxis (*Babelomurex santacruzensis*), **15**
Saul's murex (*Chicoreus saulii*), 46
scallops, 59–63
  bald scallop (*Flexopecten glaber*), **60**
  calico scallop (*Argopecten gibbus*), 59
  circular scallops, 67
  cloak scallop (*Gloripallium pallium*), **63**
  lion's paw scallop (*Nodipecten nodosus*), 59
  senatorial scallop (*Mimachlamys sentoria*), **7**
  Vermilion scallop (*Mimachlamys miniacea*), 66
scorpion conch (*Lambis scorpius*), **33**
sea slugs (nudibranchs), 21
senatorial scallop (*Mimachlamys sentoria*), **7**
shells
  of bivalves, 59
  classification of, 12–19
  collection of, 70
  of gastropods, 21
  structure of, 7–12
  uses of, 3–5
slit shells, 22
  Hirase's slit shell (*Perotrochus hirasei*), **22**
slugs, 21, 68–70
snails
  Cuban tree snail (painted polymita; *Polymita picta*), 70
  Cuvier's tropid snail (*Tropidophora cuvieriana*), 70
  land and tree, 69
  moon snail, 68
  slugs and land snails, 68–70
  see also gastropods
spider conch, 34
striped top shell (*Trochus virgatus*), **28**
sunburst star turban (*Astrea heliotropium*), **29**
sundial shells, 56, **56**

tapestry turbans (*Turbo petholatus*), **21**
tellins, 63
  foliated tellin, **63**
textile cone (*Conus textile*), **13**
thorny oysters, 63
  Atlantic (American) thorny oyster (*Spondylus americanus*), **63**
tiger cowrie, 37
top shells, 27
  ringed top shell (*Calliostoma annulatum*), **28**
  striped top shell (*Trochus virgatus*), **28**
tree snails, 68, **69**, 70
  Cuban tree snail (painted polymita; *Polymita picta*), 70
tritons (Ranellidae), 39–43, **39**
  angular triton (*Cymatium femorale*), **18**
  black-spotted triton (*Cymatium lotorium*), **43**
tropid snails, 70
tulip shells (*Fasciolaria spp.*), **10**, **15**
turbans, 27
  sunburst star turban (*Astrea heliotropium*), **29**
  tapestry turban (*Turbo petholatus*), **21**
  Yoka star turban (*Gildfordia yoka*), 27
tusk shells (scaphopods), 19

Venus comb murex (*Murex pecten*), 46
Vermilion scallop (*Mimachlamys miniacea*), 66
Victor Dan's miter (*Scabriola vicdani*), **21**
volutes, 55
  Bednall's volute (*Volutoconus bednalli*), **18**
  music volute, **54**
  Ponsonby's volute (*Festilyria ponsonbyi*), 55

wentletraps, 43
  precious wentletrap (*Epitonium scalare*), **43**
West Indian fighting conch (*Strombus pugilus*), **33**
whelks, 49
white-spotted cowrie (*Cypraea guttata*), **37**

Yoka star turban (*Gildfordia yoka*), 27